PAUL McCARTNEY
CHAOS AND CREATION IN THE BACKYARD

A Publication of

MPL COMMUNICATIONS, INC.
http://www.mplcommunications.com

Exclusively Distributed By

HAL•LEONARD®
CORPORATION
7777 W. Bluemound Rd. P.O. Box 13819 Milwaukee, WI 53213

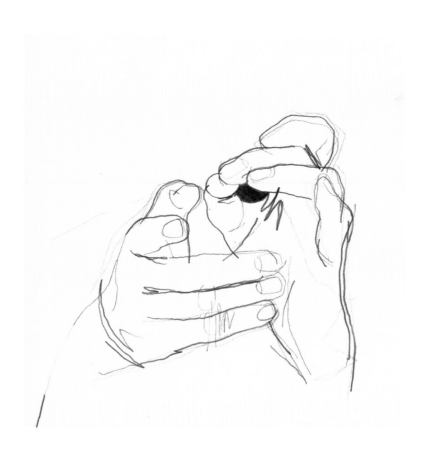

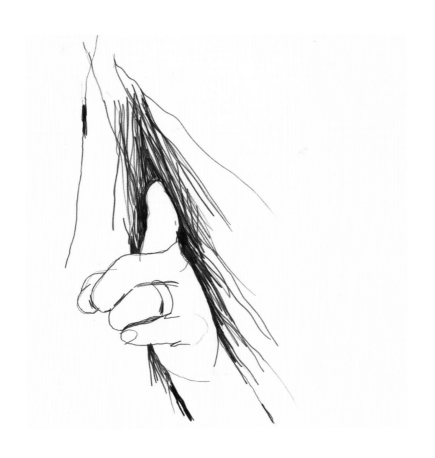
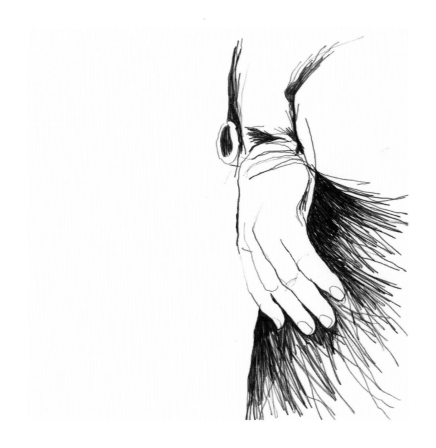

Published by MPL Communications Limited

ISBN 1-4234-0726-1
© 2005 MPL COMMUNICATIONS LTD.
Administered by MPL COMMUNICATIONS, INC.
All Rights Reserved

Music arranged by Jack Long & Derek Jones
Music processed by Paul Ewers Music Design
Cover photograph © Mike McCartney
Page 1 photograph Bill Bernstein © MPL
Line drawings © Brian Clarke

Visit Hal Leonard Online at
www.halleonard.com
www.mplcommunications.com

Fine Line

Words & Music by Paul McCartney

ci-sion makes a dif-f'rence. Get it wrong, you'd be mak-ing a big mis-take.
ev-'ry con-tri-bu - tion seems the same it's a game that you're bound to lose.

Come home bro-ther, all____ is for-giv-en. We all cried_ when you were

dri-ven a-way.____ Come home bro-ther, ev - 'ry-thing is bet-ter. Ev-

-'ry-thing is bet-ter when you come home to stay.____

11

Whatev-er's more im-por-tant to you,_____ you've got to choose what you want to do._____ What-ev-er's more im-por-tant to be,_____ well, that's the view that you got to see.__

How Kind of You

Words & Music by Paul McCartney

Some-one else_ as kind_ as you._

2. The thought-ful-ness_ you showed has made_ a dif-f'rence in my life._
3. How kind of you_ to stick by me_ dur-ing the fi-nal bout._

_ I won't for-get_ how un-a-fraid_ you
_ And lis-ten to_ the ref-er-ee_ as

were that long_ dark night._
I was count-ed out._

I thought that all was lost,_
I thought my time was up,_

How kind of you to think of me,___ how kind of you.___

Jenny Wren

Words & Music by Paul McCartney

1. Like so ma-ny girls,___ Jen-ny Wren___ could

took her song a - way.

Ooh.

At the Mercy

Words & Music by Paul McCartney

31

To Coda ⊕

Some - times I'd ra - ther run and
Some - times my head is hang - ing

hide
low,
than stay and face the fear in - side.
but it's time to get on with the show.

At the mer - cy, at the mer - cy. At the mer - cy of a bu - sy

day. Who can bear to turn their head a -

32

Friends to Go

Words & Music by Paul McCartney

for your friends to go.

2. I've been slid-ing down a slip-py slope,— I've been climb-ing up a

slow-ly burn-ing rope— but the flame is get-ting low. I've been

wait-ing on the oth-er— side— for your friends to go.—

You nev - er need to wor - ry a - bout___ me,

*2° Instrumental till ***

I'll be fine___ on my own.___

*** Some-one else can

wor - ry a - bout___ me,

I've spent a lot of time___ on my own,___

I've spent a lot of time___ on my own.___

3. I've been wait-ing till the
4. I've been wait-ing on the

37

English Tea

Words & Music by Paul McCartney

Too Much Rain

Words & Music by Paul McCartney

1. Laugh when your eyes are burn - ing.
2. You know the wheels keep turn - ing.
(3.) laugh.

Smile when your heart is filled with pain.
Why do the tears run down your face?
Smile when you're spin-ning round and round.

Sigh as you brush a-way your sor-
We used to hide a-way our feel-
Sigh as you think a-bout to-mor-

- row.
- ings.
- row.

Make a vow that it's not
But for now tell your-self
Make a vow that you're gon-

45

too much for an-y-one. Too hard for an-y-one.___ Who wants a hap-py and peace-ful life?___ 3. You've got to learn___ to

To Coda ⊕

D.S. al Coda

⊕ *Coda*

You've got to learn___ to laugh.

A Certain Softness

Words & Music by Paul McCartney

1. A cer-tain soft-ness (1, 4.) in her eyes___ fas-ci-nates me
(2.) in her smile___ cap-ti-vates me
(3.) in her style___ haunts my mem-'ry

more_ than I ev-er thought_ it would, (a cer-tain soft-ness) more_ than I ev-er thought_ it
sur- er than an-y-thing___ that's sure, (a kind of sad-ness) sur- er than an-y-thing___ be-
more_ than I ev-er thought_ it would, (a touch of wild-ness) more_ than I ev-er thought_ it

could. A cer-tain soft-ness in her eyes___ got me hooked,___
- fore. A kind of sad-ness in her smile___ got me hooked,___
could. A touch of wild-ness in her style___ got me hooked,___

4º to Coda II

50

Riding to Vanity Fair

Words & Music by Paul McCartney

1. I bit my tongue, I nev-er talked too much; I tried to be so strong.
2. You put me down but I can laugh it off and act like no-thing's wrong.

I'll use the time to think a - bout__ my - self.__

3. You're not a - ware of what you put me through; but now the feel-ing's gone.__
4. There was a time when ev - 'ry day was young; the sun would al - ways shine.__

Follow Me

Words & Music by Paul McCartney

1. You lift up my spirits, you shine on my soul,___ when-
(2.) give me di-rec-tion, you show me the way,___ you
(3.) lead me to pla-ces that I've ne-ver been,___ un-

-ev-er I'm emp-ty you make me feel whole. I can re-ly on you___ to
give me a rea-son to face ev-'ry day.___ I can de-pend on you___ to
-cov-er-ing se-crets that I've ne-ver seen.___ I can re-ly on you___ to

Promise to You Girl

Words & Music by Paul McCartney

Look - ing through the back - yard of my life:____

time to sweep the fall - en leaves a - way.

(Like the sun that ris - es ev - 'ry day,
(Ev - 'ry sin - gle se - cond of our lives

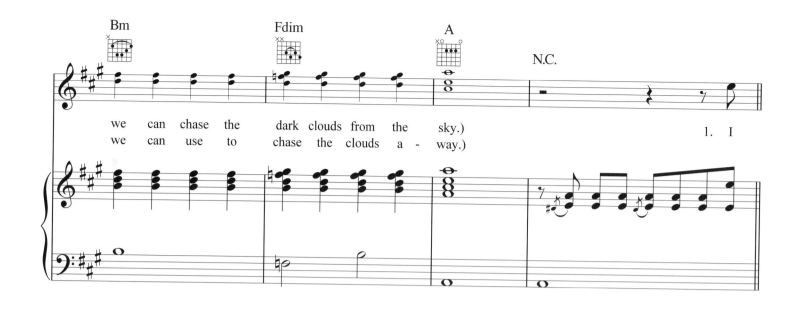

we can chase the dark clouds from the sky.)
we can use to chase the clouds a - way.)

1. I

gave my pro-mise to you, girl;
2. Hey, why wait an-oth-er day?
(3° Instrumental)
(4.) no more bark-ing up a tree,

I don't wan-na take it
That won't get us an-y-
no more how-ling at the

Optional 8vb

back.
- where.
moon.

You and me,__
All the time__
They won't see__

side by side,__
that it takes__
you and I____

(Falsetto) Ooh._____

Ooh._____

Look-ing   through   the   back - yard   of   my   life:____

time   to   sweep_   the   fall - en   leaves_   a - way.

This Never Happened Before

Words & Music by Paul McCartney

It's not so good when you're on_____ your own._____

3. So   come to me,
4. I'm   ve - ry sure

now we can be   what__ we   want to be.   I   love   you,   and
this nev - er hap - pened to   me be - fore   I   met   you,   and

To Coda ⊕

now I see   this is the way it should be._____
now I'm sure

67

Anyway

Words & Music by Paul McCartney

1. If you love me, won't you call me?
2. If we could be clos-er long-er,

I've been wait-ing, wait-ing too long. In my soul is
that would help me, help me so much. We can cure each

con-stant yearn-ing; al-ways sing-ing,___ sing-ing this song.___
oth-er's sor-row; won't you please,___ please, please___ get in touch.___

On-ly love___ is strong___ e-nough___ to take it on___ the chin.___
If a love___ is strong___ e-nough,___ it may nev-er end.___

When did I___ be-gin___ to fall?
Why would I___ pre-tend___ to fall?